LOVE SONNETS

All good wishes,
Sheish Picken

WHEN APPLES WERE GOLDEN AND SONGS WERE SWEET.
JOHN MELHUISH STRUDWICK (1849-1937)
City Art Gallery, Manchester

LOVE ⹀ ⹀
SONNETS

A Treasury of English Verse

Edited by
SHEILA PICKLES
Scented by **PENHALIGON'S**

PAVILION

FOR JANE AND ROGER – THE LOVE OF A LIFETIME

First published in Great Britain in 1995 by
Pavilion Books Limited
26 Upper Ground
London SE1 9PD

Introduction and selection copyright © 1995 by Sheila Pickles

With thanks to the Bridgeman Art Library for supplying the pictures on
the following pages: 1, 2, 3, 8, 11, 12, 15, 16, 19, 23, 24, 26, 29, 30, 33, 37,
38, 41, 42, 46, 49, 50, 52, 54, 56, 60, 62, 65.

The moral right of the author has been asserted

Designed by David Fordham

A CIP catalogue record for this book is available from the British Library.

ISBN 1-857693-1610

Typeset by SX Composing Ltd, Rayleigh, Essex
Printed in Hong Kong by Imago

2 4 6 8 10 9 7 5 3 1

This book may be ordered by post direct from the publisher. Please
contact the Marketing Department. But try your bookshop first.

PAGE 1: LORD NORTH. ISAAC OLIVER (1551-1617)
Victoria & Albert Museum, London.

PAGE 3: PORTRAIT OF MADAME RIMSKY KORSAKOV.
FRANZ XAVIER WINTERHALTER (1806-73) Musée D'Orsay, Paris.

OPPOSITE: LADY ANNE POPE. ROBERT PEAKE (C. 1551-1619)
Tate Gallery, London.

CONTENTS

Dear reader

The particular type of poem we refer to as a sonnet shares its roots with the world sonata, meaning 'sounded' or 'played', and would originally have been accompanied by a musical instrument. A sonnet is composed of fourteen lines and follows a definite structure. Its form first made its appearance in Italy at the beginning of the twelfth century where, in the following centuries, it was favoured by the great poets Dante and Petrarch. It has been a popular verse-form ever since. Sir Philip Sydney was one of the first English poets to write in sonnet verse, but it was Edmund Spenser and William Shakespeare who made the form popular in this country. Reading sonnets from the sixteenth century, I am struck by their timelessness and by their enduring beauty. The sonnet seems highly appropriate for the subject of love, its rigid format giving it an impact which longer poems often lack.

At the end of the seventeenth century, the sonnet disappeared from English poetry for nearly a hundred years and was only revived by the Romantics. In a departure from tradition, poets such as Wordsworth, Coleridge and Byron used the form to write about their social ideals and impressions as well as about love, giving a new meaning to the form. The sonnet's popularity continued into the nineteenth century, with wonderful examples by Elizabeth Barrett Browning and Dante Gabriel Rossetti.

Cynics who scorn poetry for being sentimental are nevertheless often drawn to sonnets when they fall in love, for these intimate and tightly structured poems offer the perfect means for communicating personal feelings.

SHEILA PICKLES 1995

ELIZABETHAN
SONNETS

THE MAGDALEN READING.
AMBROSIUS BENSON (FL. 1518-50)
National Gallery, London.

PORTRAIT OF EVANGELISTA SCAPPI.
FRANCESCO DI MARCO RAIBOLINI (1450-1517),
Galleria Degli Uffizi, Florence.

LOVING IN TRUTH

LOVING IN TRUTH, and fain in verse my love to show,
That she, dear she, might take some pleasure of my pain:
Pleasure might cause her read, reading might make her know,
Knowledge might pity win, and pity grace obtain,
  I sought fit words to paint the blackest face of woe,
Studying inventions fine, her wits to entertain:
Oft turning others' leaves to see if thence would flow
Some fresh and fruitful showers upon my sun-burn'd brain.
  But words came halting forth, wanting Invention's stay,
Invention, Nature's child, fled step-dame Study's blows,
And others' feet still seem'd but strangers in my way.
Thus great with child to speak, and helpless in my throes,
    Biting my trewand pen, beating myself for spite,
    Fool, said my Muse to me, look in thy heart and write.

SIR PHILIP SIDNEY, 1554-1586

WITH HOW SAD STEPS

WITH HOW SAD STEPS, O Moon, thou climb'st the skies,
  How silently, and with how wan a face,
  What, may it be that even in heav'nly place
That busy archer his sharp arrows tries?
Sure if that long with love acquainted eyes
  Can judge of love, thou feel'st a lover's case;
  I read it in thy looks, thy languish'd grace,
To me that feel the like, thy state descries.
  Then ev'n of fellowship, O Moon, tell me
Is constant love deem'd there but want of wit?
Are beauties there as proud as here they be?
Do they above love to be lov'd, and yet
  Those lovers scorn whom that love doth possess?
  Do they call virtue there ungratefulness?

SIR PHILIP SIDNEY, 1554-1586

So Oft As I Her Beauty Do Behold

So oft as I her beauty do behold,
And therewith do her cruelty compare,
I marvel of what substance was the mould
The which her made at once so cruel fair.
Not earth; for her high thoughts more heavenly are:
Not water; for her love doth burn like fire:
Not air; for she is not so light or rare:
Not fire; for she doth freeze with faint desire.
Then needs another element inquire
Whereof she mote be made; that is the sky:
For to the heaven her haughty looks aspire,
And eke her mind is pure and immortal high.
Then sith to heaven ye likenèd are the best,
Belike in mercy as in all the rest.

EDMUND SPENSER, 1552-1599

Being Myself Captivèd Here

Being myself captivèd here in care
My heart, (whom none with servile bands can tie
But the fair tresses of your golden hair)
Breaking his prison, forth to you doth fly.
Like as a bird that in one's hand doth spy.
Desired food, to it doth make his flight:
Even so my heart, that wont on your fair eye
To feed his fill, flies back unto your sight.
Do you him take, and in your bosom bright,
Gently encage, that he may be your thrall:
Perhaps he there may learn with rare delight,
To sing your name and praises over all.
That it hereafter may you not repent,
Him lodging in your bosom to have lent.

EDMUND SPENSER, 1552-1599

PORTRAIT OF A LADY AS THE MAGDALEN.
RICCI OR PEDRINI GIANPIETRINO (16TH CENTURY)
Christie's, London.

SONNET XXX FROM AMORETTI

My love is like to ice, and I to fire;
How comes it then that this her cold so great
Is not dissolved through my so hot desire,
But harder grows the more I her entreat?
Or how comes it that my exceeding heat
Is not delayed by her heart frozen cold:
But that I burn much more in boiling sweat,
And feel my flames augmented manifold?
What more miraculous thing may be told
That fire which all things melts, should harden ice?
And ice which is congealed with senseless cold
Should kindle fire by wonderful device?
  Such is the power of love in gentle mind
  That it can alter all the course of kind.

EDMUND SPENSER, 1552-1599

ABOVE: PORTRAIT OF A LADY.
ROGIER VAN DER WEYDEN (1399-1464) National Gallery, London.

OPPOSITE: UNKNOWN MAN WITH FLAME BACKGROUND.
NICHOLAS HILLIARD (1547-1619) Ham House, London.

Spring Sent to His Mistress Like a Herald

Fresh spring, the herald of love's mighty king,
In whose coat-armor richly are displayed
All sorts of flowers the which on earth do spring,
In goodly colors gloriously arrayed,
Go to my Love, where she is careless laid
Yet in her winter's bower, not well awake:
Tell her the joyous time will not be stayed,
Unless she do him by the forelock take;
Bid her therefore herself soon ready make,
To wait on Love amongst his lovely crew;
Where every one that misseth then her make,
Shall be by him amerced with penance due.
   Make haste therefore, sweet love, whilst it is prime;
   For none can call again the passéd time.

Edmund Spenser, 1552-1599

Shall I Compare Thee to a Summer's Day?

Shall I compare thee to a summer's day?
Thou art more lovely and more temperate:
Rough winds do shake the darling buds of May,
And summer's lease hath all too short a date:
Sometime too hot the eye of heaven shines,
And often is his gold complexion dimm'd;
And every fair from fair sometime declines,
By chance, or nature's changing course untrimm'd;
But thy eternal summer shall not fade,
Nor lose possession of that fair thou ow'st,
Nor shall death brag thou wander'st in his shade,
When in eternal lines to time thou grow'st,
   So long as men can breathe, or eyes can see,
   So long lives this, and this gives life to thee.

William Shakespeare, 1564-1616

THE THREE GRACES (DETAIL FROM PRIMAVERA)
SANDRO BOTTICELLI (1440-1510)
Galleria Degli Uffizi, Florence.

SELF PORTRAIT WITH ISABEL BRANDT.
PETER PAUL RUBENS (1577-1640)
Alte Pinakotheck, Munich.

True Love Not at the Mercy of Time and Circumstance

Let me not to the marriage of true minds
Admit impediments. Love is not love
Which alters when it alteration finds,
Or bends with the remover to remove.
O no; it is an ever fixéd mark,
That looks on tempests and is never shaken:
It is the star to every wandering bark,
Whose worth's unknown, although his height be taken.
Love's not Time's fool, though rosy lips and cheeks
Within his bending sickle's compass come;
Love alters not with his brief hours and weeks,
But bears it out even unto the edge of doom.
   If this be error, and upon me proved,
   I never writ, nor no man ever loved.

William Shakespeare, 1564-1616

Fortune and Men's Eyes

When, in disgrace with Fortune and men's eyes,
I all alone beweep my outcast state,
And trouble deaf heaven with my bootless cries,
And look upon myself and curse my fate,
Wishing me like to one more rich in hope,
Featured like him, like him with friends possessed,
Desiring this man's art, and that man's scope,
With what I most enjoy contented least;
Yet in these thoughts myself almost despising,
Haply I think on thee, and then my state,
Like to the lark at break of day arising
From sullen earth, sings hymns at heaven's gate;
   For thy sweet love remember'd such wealth brings,
   That then I scorn to change my state with kings.

William Shakespeare, 1564-1616

When My Love Swears

WHEN MY LOVE SWEARS that she is made of truth,
I do believe her, though I know she lies,
That she might think me some untutor'd youth,
Unlearned in the world's false subtleties.
Thus vainly thinking that she thinks me young,
Although she knows my days are past the best,
Simply I credit her false-speaking tongue;
On both sides thus is simple truth suppress'd.
But wherefore says she not she is unjust?
And wherefore say not I that I am old?
O, love's best habit is in seeming trust,
And age in love loves not to have years told.
  Therefore I lie with her, and she with me,
  And in our faults by lies we flattered be.

WILLIAM SHAKESPEARE, 1564-1616

Let Me Confess

LET ME CONFESS that we two must be twain,
Although our undivided loves are one;
So shall those blots that do with me remain,
Without thy help, by me be borne alone.
In our two loves there is but one respect,
Though in our lives a separable spite,
Which though it alter not love's sole effect,
Yet doth it steal sweet hours from love's delight.
  I may not evermore acknowledge thee,
Lest my bewailed guilt should do thee shame;
Nor thou with public kindness honour me,
Unless thou take that honour from thy name.
  But do not so; I love thee in such sort
  As, thou being mine, mine is thy good report.

WILLIAM SHAKESPEARE, 1564-1616

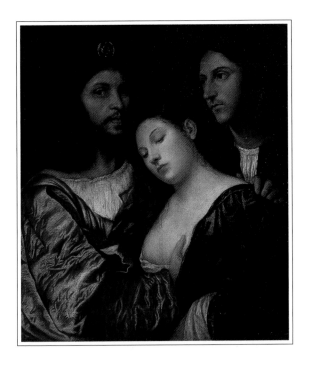

SEDUCTION.
ITALIAN SCHOOL (16TH CENTURY)
Casa Buonarroti, Florence.

LADY ELIZABETH POPE.
ATTRIB. ROBERT PEAKE (C.1551-1619)
Tate Gallery, London.

My Mistress' Eyes

My mistress' eyes are nothing like the sun;
Coral is far more red than her lips' red;
If snow be white, why then her breasts are dun;
If hairs be wires, black wires grow on her head.
I have seen roses damasked, red and white,
But no such roses see I in her cheeks,
And in some perfumes is there more delight
Than in the breath that from my mistress reeks.
I love to hear her speak, yet well I know
That music hath a far more pleasing sound.
I grant I never saw a goddess go;
My mistress when she walks treads on the ground.
    And yet, by heaven, I think my love as rare
    As any she belied with false compare.

WILLIAM SHAKESPEARE, 1564-1616

No Longer Mourn for Me

No longer mourn for me when I am dead
Than you shall hear the surly sullen bell
Give warning to the world that I am fled
From this vile world, with vilest worms to dwell.
Nay, if you read this line, remember not
The hand that writ it; for I love you so,
That I in your sweet thoughts would be forgot,
If thinking on me then should make you woe.
O, if, I say, you look upon this verse,
When I perhaps compounded am with clay,
Do not so much as my poor name rehearse,
But let your love even with my life decay;
    Lest the wise world should look into your moan,
    And mock you with me after I am gone.

WILLIAM SHAKESPEARE, 1564-1616

THE STAR OF MY MISHAP

THE STAR OF MY MISHAP imposed my paining
To spend the April of my years in crying;
That never found my fortune but in waning,
With still fresh cares my blood and body trying.
Yet her I blame not, though she might have blest me;
But my Desire's wings so high aspiring:
Now melted with the sun that hath possest me
Down do I fall from off my high desiring.
And in my fall do cry for mercy speedy,
No piteous eye looks back upon my mourning;
No help I find, when now most favour need I:
My ocean tears drown me, and quench my burning.   SAMUEL
   And this my death must christen her anew,   DANIEL,
   Whiles faith doth bid my cruel Fair "Adieu"!   1562-1619

FROM 'HYMEN'S TRIUMPH'

AH! I REMEMBER WELL (and how can I
But evermore remember well) when first
Our flame began, when scarce we knew what was
The flame we felt; when as we sat and sighed
And looked upon each other, and conceived
Not what we ail'd, – yet something we did ail;
And yet were well, and yet we were not well,
And what was our disease we could not tell.
Then would we kiss, then sigh, then look; and thus
In that first garden of our simpleness
We spent our childhood. But when years began
To reap the fruit of knowledge, ah, how then
Would she with graver looks, with sweet stern brow
Check my presumption and my forwardness;
   Yet still would give me flowers, still would me show
   What she would have me, yet not have me know.

SAMUEL DANIEL, 1562-1619

22

PORTRAIT OF ISABELLA DE MEDICI.
AGNOLO BRONZINO (1503-72)
Galleria Degli Uffizi, Florence.

HENRY PERCY, 9TH EARL OF NORTHUMBERLAND.
NICHOLAS HILLIARD (1547-1619)
Rijksmuseum, Amsterdam.

Restore thy Tresses

Restore thy tresses to the golden ore,
Yield Cytherea's son those arks of love;
Bequeath the heavens the stars that I adore,
And to the Orient do thy pearls remove.
Yield thy hand's pride unto the ivory white,
To Arabian odours give thy breathing sweet;
Restore thy blush unto Aurora bright,
To Thetis give the honour of thy feet.
Let Venus have the graces she resigned,
And thy sweet voice give back unto the spheres:
But yet restore thy fierce and cruel mind
To Hyrcan tigers and to ruthless bears.
  Yield to the marble thy hard heart again;
  So shalt thou cease to plague, and I to pain.

SAMUEL DANIEL, 1562-1619

To the Nightingale

O nightingale, that on yon bloomy spray
Warblest at eve, when all the woods are still,
Thou with fresh hope the lover's heart dost fill,
While the jolly hours lead on propitious May;
Thy liquid notes that close the eye of day,
First heard before the shallow cuckoo's bill,
Portend success in love; O if Jove's will
Have linked that amorous power to thy soft lay,
Now timely sing, ere the rude bird of hate
Foretell my hopeless doom in some grove nigh;
As thou from year to year hast sung too late
For my relief, yet hadst no reason why:
Whether the Muse, or Love call thee his mate,
Both them I serve, and of their train am I.

JOHN MILTON, 1608-1674

GEORGE GRISZE.
HANS HOLBEIN (1497/8-1543)
Staatliche Gemalde-Galerie, Berlin.

To His Mistress Objecting to Him Neither Toying Nor Talking

YOU SAY I LOVE NOT, 'cause I do not play
Still with your curls, and kiss the time away.
You blame me too, because I can't devise
Some sport to please those babies in your eyes:
By love's religion, I must here confess it,
The most I love when I the least express it.
Small griefs find tongues: full casks are ever found
To give (if any, yet) but little sound.
Deep waters noiseless are: and this we know,
That chiding streams betray small depth below.
So, when love speechless is, she doth express
A depth in love and that depth bottomless.
Now, since my love is tongueless, know me such
Who speak but little 'cause I love so much.

ROBERT HERRICK, 1591-1674

No Loathsomeness in Love

WHAT I FANCY, I approve,
No dislike there is in love:
Be my Mistress short or tall,
And distorted therewithal:
Be she likewise one of those,
That an acre hath of nose:
Be her forehead, and her eyes
Full of incongruities:
Be her cheeks so shallow too,
As to shew her tongue wag through:
Be her lips ill hung, or set,
And her grinders black as jet;
Has she thin hair, hath she none,
She's to me a paragon.

ROBERT HERRICK, 1591-1674

DEAR

Dear! why should you command me to my rest,
When now the night doth summon all to sleep?
Methinks, this time becometh lovers best!
Night was ordained, together friends to keep.
How happy are all other living things,
Which, through the day, disjoined by several flight,
The quiet evening yet together brings,
And each returns unto his Love at night!
O thou that art so courteous else to all,
Why shouldst thou, Night, abuse me only thus,
That every creature to his kind dost call,
And yet 'tis thou dost only sever us?
   Well could I wish, it would be ever day;
   If, when night comes, you bid me go away!

MICHAEL DRAYTON, 1563-1631

BRIGHT STAR OF BEAUTY

Bright star of beauty, on whose eyelids sit
A thousand nymph-like and enamoured graces,
The goddesses of memory and wit,
Which there in order take their several places,
In whose dear bosom sweet delicious Love
Lays down his quiver which he once did bear,
Since he that blessèd paradise did prove,
And leaves his mother's lap to sport him there;
Let others strive to entertain with words –
My soul is of a braver metal made;
I hold that vile, which vulgar wit affords;
In me's that faith which time cannot invade.
Let what I praise be still made good by you:
Be you most worthy, whilst I am most true.

MICHAEL DRAYTON, 1563-1631

LUCREZIA PANCIATICHI.
AGNOLO BRONZINO (1503-72)
Galleria Degli Uffizi, Florence.

MARY QUEEN OF SCOTS.
ANON.
Victoria & Albert Museum, London.

Trust Not, Sweet Soul

Trust not, sweet soul, those curled waves of gold,
With gentle tides which on your temples flow,
Nor temples spread with flakes of virgin snow,
Nor snow of cheeks with Tyrian grain enroll'd;
Trust not those shining lights which wrought my woe,
When first I did their burning rays behold,
Nor voice, whose sounds more strange effects do show
Than of the Thracian harper have been told.
Look to this dying lily, fading rose,
Dark hyacinth, of late whose blushing beams
Made all the neighbouring herbs and grass rejoice,
And think how little is 'twixt life's extremes:
    The cruel tyrant that did kill those flow'rs,
    Shall once, ay me! not spare that spring of yours.

WILLIAM DRUMMOND OF HAWTHORNDEN, 1585-1649

My Love for Him is Growing

My love for him is growing and shall grow
Throughout my life as long as there's a part
Where it can grow to greatness in that heart;
Then at the last my love may show
So very clearly he shall have no doubt.
For him I'll undergo the worst ordeal.
For him, I'll seek out honour with all zeal.
And through my deeds for certain he'll find out
That wealth, content and ease are lost to me
Unless I do his will and serve him loyally.
For him, I seek good chance from fortune's store.
For him, I wish to keep my life and thrive;
For him, to follow virtue's path I'll strive;
And he will find me constant evermore.

MARY, QUEEN OF SCOTS, 1542-1587

FAIR IS MY LOVE

FAIR IS MY LOVE that feeds among the lilies,
   The lilies growing in the pleasant garden,
Where Cupid's mount, that well-beloved hill is,
   And where that little god himself is warden.
See where my love sits in the beds of spices,
   Beset all round with camphor, myrrh and roses,
And interlac'd with curious devices,
   Which her from all the world apart incloses.
There doth she tune her lute for her delight,
   And with sweet music makes the ground to move,
Whilst I (poor I) do sit in heavy plight,
   Wailing alone my unrespected love,
Not daring to rush into so rare a place,
That gives to her, and she to it, a grace.

BARTHOLOMEW GRIFFIN, D. 1602

CUPID AND CAMPASPE

CUPID and my Campaspe played
At cards for kisses, Cupid paid;
He stakes his quiver, bow, and arrows,
His mother's doves, and team of sparrows;
Loses them too; then, down he throws
The coral of his lip, the rose
Growing on's cheek (but none knows how);
With these, the crystal of his brow,
And then the dimple of his chin:
All these did my Campaspe win.
At last, he set her both his eyes;
She won, and Cupid blind did rise.
   O Love! has she done this to thee?
   What shall (alas!) become of me?

JOHN LYLY, 1554-1606

32

ROMANTIC
SONNETS

PORTRAIT OF JUSTINIA HILTON (NÉE KENT).
WILLIAM HILTON (1752-1822)
Usher Gallery, Lincolnshire County Council.

Young Italian Girl by the Well.
Franz Xavier Winterhalter (1805-73)
Augustinermuseum, Freiburg.

The Holiness of Childhood

It is a beauteous evening, calm and free;
The holy time is quiet as a nun
Breathless with adoration; the broad sun
Is sinking down in its tranquillity;
The gentleness of heaven is on the sea.
Listen! the mighty Being is awake,
And doth with his eternal motion make
A sound like thunder – everlastingly.
Dear Child! dear Girl! that walkest with me here,
If thou appear'st untouched by solemn thought,
Thy nature is not therefore less divine:
Thou liest in Abraham's bosom all the year;
And worshipp'st at the Temple's inner shrine,
God being with thee when we know it not.

William Wordsworth, 1770-1850

Placid Objects of Contemplation

Not Love, not War, nor the tumultuous swell
Of civil conflict, nor the wrecks of change,
Nor Duty struggling with afflictions strange,
Not these alone inspire the tuneful shell;
But where untroubled peace and concord dwell,
There also is the Muse not loath to range,
Watching the twilight smoke of cot or grange
Skyward ascending from a woody dell.
Meek aspirations please her, lone endeavor,
And sage content, and placid melancholy;
She loves to gaze upon a crystal river,
Diaphanous, because it travels slowly.
Soft is the music that would charm forever;
The flower of sweetest smell is shy and lowly.

William Wordsworth, 1770-1850

LOVE

Love, dearest Lady, such as I would speak,
Lives not within the humor of the eye; –
Not being but an outward phantasy,
That skims the surface of a tinted cheek.
Else it would wane with beauty, and grow weak, –
As if the rose made summer, – and so lie
Amongst the perishable things that die,
Unlike the love which I would give and seek,
Whose health is of no hue to feel decay
With cheeks' decay, that have a rosy prime.
Love is its own great loveliness alway,
And takes new lustre from the touch of time;
Its bough owns no December and no May,
But bears its blossom into Winter's clime.

THOMAS HOOD, 1798-1845

TO MY WIFE

(On Modelling my Bust.)

Ah, Marian mine, the face you look on now
    Is not exactly like my wedding day's;
    Sunk is its cheek, deeper-retired its gaze,
    Less white and smooth its temple-flattened brow.
Sorrow has been there with his silent plough,
    And strait, stern hand. No matter, if it raise
    Aught that affection fancies, it may praise,
    Or make me worthier of Apollo's bough.
Loss, after all – such loss especially –
    Is transfer, change, but not extinction, – no;
    Part in our children's apple cheeks I see;
And, for the rest, while you look at me so,
    Take care you do not smile it back to me,
    And miss the copied furrows as you go.

JAMES HENRY LEIGH HUNT, 1784-1859

PORTRAIT OF A LADY SEATED AND HER HUSBAND STANDING.
ATTRIB. HENRY SINGLETON (1766-1839)
Christie's, London.

COURTSHIP IN THE PARK.
JOHN OPIE (1761-1807)
National Trust of Scotland, Edinburgh.

NYMPH

NYMPH of the downward smile and sidelong glance,
In what diviner moments of the day
Art thou most lovely? – When gone far astray
Into the labyrinths of sweet utterance?
Or when serenely wand'ring in a trance
Of sober thought? Or when starting away
With careless robe to meet the morning ray
Thou spar'st the flowers in thy mazy dance?
Haply 'tis when thy ruby lips part sweetly,
And so remain, because thou listenest:
But thou to please wert nurtured so completely
That I can never tell what mood is best.
   I shall as soon pronounce which Grace more neatly
   Trips it before Apollo than the rest.

JOHN KEATS, 1795-1821

I CRY YOUR MERCY, PITY, LOVE

I CRY YOUR MERCY, pity, love – aye love!
   Merciful love that tantalizes not
One-thoughted, never-wandering, guileless love,
   Unmasked, and being seen – without a blot!
Oh, let me have thee whole, – all, all, be mine!
   That shape, that fairness, that sweet minor zest
Of love, your kiss – those hands, those eyes divine,
   That warm, white, lucent, million-pleasured breast;
Yourself – your soul – in pity give me all,
   Withhold no atom's atom or I die;
Or living on, perhaps, your wretched thrall,
   Forget, in the midst of idle misery,
Life's purposes – the palate of my mind
Losing its gust, and my ambition blind!

JOHN KEATS, 1795-1821

His Last Sonnet

Bright Star! would I were steadfast as thou art!
   Not in lone splendor hung aloft the night,
And watching, with eternal lids apart,
   Like Nature's patient sleepless Eremite,
The moving waters at their priestlike task
   Of pure ablution round earth's human shores,
Or gazing on the new soft-fallen mask
   Of snow upon the mountains and the moors:
No! yet still steadfast, still unchangeable,
   Pillowed upon my fair love's ripening breast,
To feel forever its soft fall and swell,
   Awake forever in a sweet unrest,
Still, still to hear her tender-taken breath,
And so live ever, or else swoon to death.

JOHN KEATS, 1795-1821

The Lover Left by His Love at Evening

The day is gone, and all its sweets are gone!
   Sweet voice, sweet lips, soft hands, and softer breast,
Warm breath, light whisper, tender semitone,
   Bright eyes, accomplished shape, and lang'rous waist!
Faded the flower and all its budded charms;
   Faded the sight of beauty from my eyes;
Faded the shape of beauty from my arms;
   Faded the voice, warmth, whiteness, paradise –
Vanished unseasonably at shut of eve,
   When the dusk holiday – or holinight –
Of fragrant-curtained love begins to weave
   The woof of darkness thick, for hid delight;
But, as I've read love's missal through to-day,
He'll let me sleep, seeing I fast and pray.

JOHN KEATS, 1795-1821

Woman at Her Toilet.
Francois Boucher (1703-70)
Agnew & Sons, London.

PORTRAIT OF MADAME GUIMARD.
JACQUES LOUIS DAVID (1748-1825)
Private Collection.

SUMMER

THE SUMMER, the divinest Summer burns;
　　The skies are bright with azure and with gold;
The mavis and the nightingale, by turns,
　　Amid the woods a soft enchantment hold;
The flowering woods, with glory and delight,
　　Their tender leaves unto the air have spread;
The wanton air, amid their valleys bright,
　　Doth softly fly, and a light fragrance shed;
The nymphs within the silver fountains play,
　　And angels on the golden banks recline
Wherein great Flora, in her bright array,
　　Hath sprinkled her ambrosial sweets divine:
Or, else, I gaze upon that beauteous face,
O Amoret! and think these sweets have place.

LORD THURLOW, 1781-1829

TO MY WIFE

THE BUTTERFLY, which sports on gaudy wing;
　　The brawling brooklet, lost in foam and spray,
　　As it goes dancing on its idle way;
　　The sunflower, in broad daylight glistening;
Are types of her who in the festive ring
　　Lives but to bask in fashion's vain display,
　　And glittering through her bright but useless day,
　　"Flaunts, and goes down a disregarded thing!"
Thy emblem, Lucy, is the busy bee,
　　Whose industry for future hours provides;
　　The gentle streamlet, gladding as it glides
Unseen along; the flower which gives the lea
　　Fragrance and loveliness, are types of thee,
　　And of the active worth thy modest merit hides.

BERNARD BARTON (?)

Heavenly and Earthly Beauty Combined

THY CHEEK IS PALE with thought, but not from woe,
   And yet so lovely that if mirth could flush
   Its rose of whiteness with the brightest blush,
My heart would wish away that ruder glow; –
And dazzle not thy deep blue eyes, – but oh!
   While gazing on them sterner eyes will gush,
   And into mine my mother's weakness rush,
Soft as the last drops round heaven's airy bow.
For, though thy long dark lashes, low depending,
   The soul of melancholy gentleness
Gleams like a seraph from the sky descending,
   Above all pain, yet pitying all distress;
At once such majesty with sweetness blending,
   I worship more, but cannot love thee less.

LORD BYRON, 1788-1824

Sonnet, to Genevra

THINE EYES' BLUE TENDERNESS, thy long fair hair,
   And the wan lustre of thy features – caught
   From contemplation – where serenely wrought,
Seems Sorrow's softness charm'd from its despair –
Have thrown such speaking sadness in thine air,
   That – but I know thy blessed bosom fraught
   With mines of unalloy'd and stainless thought –
I should have deem'd thee doom'd to earthly care.
With such an aspect, by his colours blent,
   When from his beauty-breathing pencil born
(Except that *thou* hast nothing to repent),
   The Magdalen of Guido saw the morn –
Such seem'st thou – but how much more excellent!
   With nought Remorse can claim – nor virtue scorn.

LORD BYRON, 1788-1824

HENRIETTE DE VERNINAC.
JACQUES LOUIS DAVID (1748-1825)
The Louvre, Paris.

THE YOUNG LOVERS.
GERARD HOET (1648-1733)
Hayes Fine Art, Broadway, Worcester.

FAREWELL TO LOVE

FAREWELL, SWEET LOVE! yet blame you not my truth:
   More fondly ne'er did mother eye her child
   Than I your form. *Yours* were my hopes of youth,
   And as *you* shaped my thoughts, I sighed or smiled.
While most were wooing wealth, or gayly swerving
   To pleasure's secret haunts, and some apart
   Stood strong in pride, self-conscious of deserving,
   To you I gave my whole, weak, wishing heart.
And when I met the maid that realized
   Your fair creations, and had won her kindness,
   Say but for her if aught in earth I prized!
Your dream alone I dreamt, and caught your blindness.
   O grief! – but farewell, Love! I will go play me
   With thoughts that please me less, and less betray me.

SAMUEL TAYLOR COLERIDGE, 1772-1834

TO HOPE

O EVER SKILLED TO WEAR the form we love!
   To bid the shapes of fear and grief depart;
Come, gentle Hope! with one gay smile remove
   The lasting sadness of an aching heart.
Thy voice, benign enchantress! let me hear;
   Say that for me some pleasures yet shall bloom,
That fancy's radiance, friendship's precious tear,
   Shall soften, or shall chase, misfortune's gloom.
But come not glowing in the dazzling ray
   Which once with dear illusions charmed my eye;
O, strew no more, sweet flatterer! on my way
   The flowers I fondly thought too bright to die:
Visions less fair will soothe my pensive breast,
That asks not happiness, but longs for rest.

HELEN MARIA WILLIAMS (?)

NIGHT

THE CRACKLING EMBERS on the hearth are dead;
The indoor note of industry is still;
The latch is fast; upon the window sill
The small birds wait not for their daily bread;
The voiceless flowers – how quietly they shed
Their nightly odours; – and the household rill
Murmurs continuous dulcet sounds that fill
The vacant expectation, and the dread
Of listening night. And haply now She sleeps;
For all the garrulous noises of the air
Are hushed in peace; the soft dew silent weeps,
Like hopeless lovers for a maid so fair –
Oh! that I were the happy dream that creeps
To her soft heart, to find my image there.

HARTLEY COLERIDGE, 1796-1849

TO MARY UNWIN

MARY! I WANT A LYRE with other strings;
Such aid from heaven as some have feigned they drew,
An eloquence scarce given to mortals, new
And undebased by praise of meaner things,
That ere through age or woe I shed my wings,
I may record thy worth with honour due,
In verse as musical as thou art true,
And that immortalizes whom it sings; –
But thou hast little need. There is a Book
By seraphs writ with beams of heavenly light,
On which the eyes of God not rarely look,
A chronicle of actions just and bright –
There all thy deeds, my faithful Mary, shine;
And since thou own'st that praise, I spare thee mine.

WILLIAM COWPER, 1731-1800

READING BY A PAPER BELL SHADE.
HENRY ROBERT MORLAND (1730-97)
Agnew & Sons, London.

SHEPHERD PIPING TO A SHEPHERDESS.
FRANCOIS BOUCHER (1703-70)
Wallace Collection, London.

An Invitation

LADY, I BID THEE to a sunny dome,
Ringing with echoes of Italian song:
Henceforth to thee these magic halls belong,
And all the pleasant place is like a home.
Hark, on the right with full piano tone
Old Dante's voice encircles all the air;
Hark yet again, like flute-notes mingling rare,
Comes the keen sweetness of Petrarca's moan.
Pass thou the lintel freely; without fear
Feast on the music. I do better know thee,
Than to suspect this pleasure thou dost owe me
Will wrong thy gentle spirit, or make less dear
That element whence thou must draw thy life, –
An English maiden and an English wife.

ARTHUR H. HALLAM, 1811-1833

A Lover's Wish

OH BLESSING AND DELIGHT of my young heart,
Maiden who was so lovely and so pure,
I know not in what region now thou art,
Or whom thy gentle eyes in joy assure.
Not the old hills on which we gazed together,
Not the old faces which we both did love,
Not the old books whence knowledge we did gather,
Not these, but others now thy fancies move.
I would I knew thy present hopes and fears,
All thy companions, with their pleasant talk,
And the clear aspect which thy dwelling wears;
So, though in body absent, I might walk
With thee in thought and feeling, till thy mood
Did sanctify mine own to peerless good.

ARTHUR H. HALLAM, 1811-1833

51

ELIZABETH OF BAVARIA.
FRANZ XAVIER WINTERHALTER (1806-73)
Kunsthistorisches Museum, Vienna.

REASONS FOR BEING BELOVED

THE REASON WHY WE LOVE THEE, dost thou ask?
We love for many reasons joined in one: –
Because thy face is fair to look upon;
Because, when pains or toils our hearts o'ertask,
In sunny smiles of thine they love to bask;
Because thou honorest all, and harmest none;
Because thy froward moods so soon are gone;
Thy many faults and foibles wear no mask;
Because thou art a woman. Unto me
A gracious woman is a child mature;
Docile, and gentle, though with many a lure
Enriched, and, in a soft subjection free;   AUBREY DE VERE,
A sanguine creature, full of winning ways;   THE YOUNGER,
Athirst for love, and shyly pleased with praise.   1788-1846

VICTORIAN SONNETS

A READER.
ALBERT JOSEPH MOORE (1841-93)
City Art Gallery, Manchester.

Summer Evening at Skagen, the Artist's Wife
with a Dog on the Beach.
Peter Severin Kroyer (1851-1909) Skagens Museum, Denmark.

How Do I Love Thee?

How do I love thee? Let me count the ways.
I love thee to the depth and breadth and height
My soul can reach, when feeling out of sight
For the ends of Being and ideal Grace.
I love thee to the level of everyday's
Most quiet need, by sun and candle-light.
I love thee freely, as men strive for Right;
I love thee purely, as they turn from Praise;
I love thee with the passion put to use
In my old griefs, and with my childhood's faith.
I love thee with a love I seemed to lose
With my lost saints, – I love thee with the breath,
Smiles, tears, of all my life! – and, if God choose,
I shall but love thee better after death.

Elizabeth Barrett Browning, 1809-1861

If Thou Must Love Me

If thou must love me, let it be for nought
Except for love's sake only. Do not say,
'I love her for her smile – her look – her way
Of speaking gently, – for a trick of thought
That falls in well with mine, and certes brought
A sense of pleasant ease on such a day.' –
For these things in themselves, Belovèd, may
Be changed, or change for thee, – and love, so wrought
May be unwrought so. Neither love me for
Thine own dear pity's wiping my cheeks dry, –
A creature might forget to weep who bore
Thy comfort long, and lose thy love thereby!
But love me for love's sake, that evermore
Thou may'st love on, through love's eternity.

Elizabeth Barrett Browning, 1806-1861

THE KISS.
GRACE BALDRY (FL.1897)
Simon Carter Gallery, Woodbridge.

FUTURITY

AND, O BELOVED VOICES, upon which
Ours passionately call because erelong
Ye brake off in the middle of that song
We sang together softly, to enrich
The poor world with the sense of love, and witch
The heart out of things evil, – I am strong,
Knowing ye are not lost for aye among
The hills, with last year's thrush. God keeps a niche
In Heaven, to hold our idols: and albeit
He brake them to our faces and denied
That our close kisses should impair their white,
I know we shall behold them raised, complete,
The dust swept from their beauty, – glorified
New Memnons singing in the great God-light.

ELIZABETH BARRETT BROWNING, 1809-1861

NOW

OUT OF YOUR WHOLE LIFE give but a moment!
All of your life that has gone before,
All to come after it, – so you ignore,
So you make perfect the present, – condense,
In a rapture of rage, for perfection's endowment,
Thought and feeling and soul and sense –
Merged in a moment which gives me at last
You around me for once, you beneath me, above me –
Me – sure that despite of time future, time past, –
This tick of our life-time's one moment you love me!
How long such suspension may linger? Ah, Sweet –
The moment eternal – just that and no more –
When ecstasy's utmost we clutch at the core
While cheeks burn, arms open, eyes shut and lips meet!

ROBERT BROWNING, 1812-1889

HER LOVE

She loves him; for her infinite soul is Love,
   And he her lodestar. Passion in her is
   A glass facing his fire, where the bright bliss
Is mirrored, and the heat returned. Yet move
That glass, a stranger's amorous flame to prove,
   And it shall turn, by instant contraries,
   Ice to the moon; while her pure fire to his
For whom it burns, clings close i' the heart's alcove.

Lo! They are one. With wifely breast to breast
   And circling arms, she welcomes all command
   Of love, – her soul to answering ardours fann'd:
Yet as morn springs or twilight sinks to rest,
Ah! who shall say she deems not loveliest
   The hour of sisterly sweet hand-in-hand?

DANTE GABRIEL ROSSETTI, 1828-1882

ABOVE: GIRL WITH A LUTE.
JOHN MELHUISH STRUDWICK (1847-1937)
Phillips, The International Fine Art Auctioneers.

OPPOSITE: DAY DREAM.
DANTE GABRIEL ROSSETTI (1828-82)
Victoria & Albert Museum, London.

VENUS VERTICORDIA.
DANTE GABRIEL ROSSETTI (1828-82)
Russell Cotes Art Gallery and Museum, Bournemouth.

LOVE'S BAUBLES

I STOOD WHERE LOVE in brimming armfuls bore
 Slight wanton flowers and foolish toys of fruit:
 And round him ladies thronged in warm pursuit,
Fingered and lipped and proffered the strange store.
And from one hand the petal and the core
 Savoured of sleep; and cluster and curled shoot
 Seemed from another hand like shame's salute, –
Gifts that I felt my cheek was blushing for.

At last Love bade my Lady give the same:
 And as I looked, the dew was light thereon;
 And as I took them, at her touch they shone
With inmost heaven-hue of the heart of flame.
 And then Love said: "Lo! when the hand is hers,
 Follies of love are love's true ministers."

DANTE GABRIEL ROSSETTI, 1828-1882

A SONNET IS A MOMENT'S MONUMENT

A SONNET IS A MOMENT'S MONUMENT, –
 Memorial from the Soul's eternity
 To one dead deathless hour. Look that it be,
Whether for lustral rite or dire portent,
Of its own arduous fulness reverent:
 Carve it in ivory or in ebony,
 As Day or Night may rule; and let Time see
Its flowering crest impearled and orient.

A Sonnet is a coin: its face reveals
 The soul, – its converse, to what Power 'tis due: –
Whether for tribute to the august appeals
 Of Life, or dower in Love's high retinue, DANTE GABRIEL
It serve; or, 'mid the dark wharf's cavernous breath, ROSSETTI,
In Charon's palm it pay the toll to Death. 1828-1882

61

CHRYSANTHEMUMS.
JAMES JACQUES TISSOT (1836-1902)
Christopher Wood Gallery, London.

Remember

Remember me when I am gone away,
    Gone far away into the silent land;
    When you can no more hold me by the hand,
Nor I half turn to go yet turning stay.
Remember me when no more day by day
    You tell me of our future that you planned:
    Only remember me; you understand
It will be late to counsel then or pray.
Yet if you should forget me for a while
    And afterwards remember, do not grieve:
    For if the darkness and corruption leave
    A vestige of the thoughts that once I had,
Better by far you should forget and smile
    Than that you should remember and be sad.

CHRISTINA ROSSETTI, 1830-1894

To Love and to Remember

To love and to remember; that is good:
    To love and to forget; that is not well:
    To lapse from love to hatred; that is hell
And death and torment, rightly understood.
Soul dazed by love and sorrow, cheer thy mood;
    More blest art thou than mortal tongue can tell:
    Ring not thy funeral but thy marriage bell,
And salt with hope thy life's insipid food.
Love is the goal, love is the way we wend,
    Love is our parallel unending line
    Whose only perfect Parallel is Christ,
Beginning not begun, End without end:
    For He Who hath the Heart of God sufficed,
    Can satisfy all hearts, – yea, thine and mine.

CHRISTINA ROSSETTI, 1830-1894

The Four Princesses at Wilna
A Photograph

Sweet faces, that from pictured casements lean
    As from a castle window, looking down
    On some gay pageant passing through a town,
    Yourselves the fairest figures in the scene;
With what a gentle grace, with what serene
    Unconsciousness ye wear the triple crown
    Of youth and beauty and the fair renown
    Of a great name, that ne'er hath tarnished been!
From your soft eyes, so innocent and sweet,
    Four spirits, sweet and innocent as they,
    Gaze on the world below, the sky above;
Hark! there is some one singing in the street;
    'Faith, Hope, and Love! these three,' he seems to say;
    'These three; and greatest of the three is Love.'

Longfellow, 1807-1882

The Evening Star

Lo! in the painted oriel of the West,
    Whose panes the sunken sun incarnadines,
    Like a fair lady at her casement, shines
    The evening star, the star of love and rest!
And then anon she doth herself divest
    Of all her radiant garments, and reclines
    Behind the sombre screen of yonder pines,
    With slumber and soft dreams of love oppressed.
O my beloved, my sweet Hesperus!
    My morning and my evening star of love!
    My best and gentlest lady! even thus,
As that fair planet in the sky above,
    Dost thou retire unto thy rest at night,
    And from thy darkened window fades the light.

Longfellow, 1807-1882

THE BALCONY.
EUGENE BLAAS (B.1843)
Christie's, London.

PORTRAIT OF FURSTIN SUSUPOLT.
KAY ROBERTSON (FL.1892)
Pushkin Museum, Moscow.

O Beauty

O beauty, passing beauty! sweetest Sweet!
  How canst thou let me waste my youth in sighs?
I only ask to sit beside thy feet.
  Thou knowest I dare not look into thine eyes.
Might I but kiss thy hand! I dare not fold
  My arms about thee – scarcely dare to speak.
And nothing seems to me so wild and bold,
  As with one kiss to touch thy blessèd cheek.
Methinks if I should kiss thee, no control
  Within the thrilling brain could keep afloat
    The subtle spirit. Even while I spoke,
The bare word KISS hath made my inner soul
    To tremble like a lute-string, ere the note
    Hath melted in the silence that it broke.

ALFRED LORD TENNYSON, 1809-1892

O, Were I Loved as I Desire to Be!

O, were I loved as I desire to be!
  What is there in the great sphere of the earth,
  Or range of evil between death and birth,
  That I should fear, – if I were loved by thee?
All the inner, all the outer world of pain,
  Clear love would pierce and cleave, if thou wert mine;
  As I have heard that somewhere in the main
  Fresh-water springs come up through bitter brine.
'T were joy, not fear, clasped hand in hand with thee,
  To wait for death – mute – careless of all ills,
  Apart upon a mountain, though the surge
Of some new deluge from a thousand hills
  Flung leagues of roaring foam into the gorge
  Below us, as far on as eye could see.

ALFRED LORD TENNYSON, 1809-1892

What a Royalty of Song

Oh, what a royalty of song should greet
The unclouded advent of thy natal day!
All things of musical utterance should meet
In concord of a many-sounding lay;
Let the proud trumpet tongue thy noble praise,
The rolling drum reverberate thy fame,
Let fifes and flutes their fluttering voices raise,
And the glad cymbals tinkle to thy name;
Let the clear horn pay tribute to thy truth,
The deep-based viol tenderly intone
Thy womanly pity and large heart of ruth;
But of my love let my voice sing alone:
Theme to my jealous lips most dear, most meet,
If that my voice, to voice it, were more sweet.

JULIAN FANE, 1827-1870

Music, and Frankincense of Flowers

Music, and frankincense of flowers, belong
To this sweet festival of all the year.
Take then the latest blossom of my song,
And to Love's canticle incline thine ear.
What is it that Love chaunts? thy perfect praise.
What is it that Love prays? worthy to prove.
What is it Love desires? thy length of days.
What is it that Love asks? return of love.
Ah, what requital can Love ask more dear
Than by Love's priceless self to be repaid?
Thy liberal love, increasing year by year,
Hath granted more than all my heart hath prayed,
And, prodigal as Nature, makes me pine
To think how poor my love compared with thine.

JULIAN FANE, 1827-1870

A Sonata of Beethoven.
Alfred Edward Emslie (1848-1918)
Guildhall Art Gallery, London.

A LOVER'S FEAR

LIKE A MUSICIAN that with flying finger
Startles the voice of some new instrument,
And though he know that in one string are blent
All its extremes of sound, yet still doth linger
Among the lighter threads, fearing to start
The deep soul of that one melodious wire,
Lest it, unanswering, dash his high desire,
And spoil the hopes of his expectant heart; –
Thus, with my mistress oft conversing, I
Stir every lighter theme with careless voice,
Gathering sweet music and celestial joys
From the harmonious soul o'er which I fly;
Yet o'er the one deep master-chord I hover,
And dare not stoop, fearing to tell – I love her.

WILLIAM CALDWELL ROSCOE, 1823-1859

TO MY MOTHER

AS WINTER in some mild autumnal days,
Breathes such an air as youngest spring discloses,
So age in thee renews an infant's grace,
And clothes thy cheek in soft November roses.
Time hath made friends with Beauty in thy face,
And since the wheeling Fates must be obeyed,
White rime upon thy gracious head he lays,
But whispers gently not to be afraid;
And tenderly, like one that leads the blind,
He soothes thy lingering footsteps to the gate,
While that great Angel, who there keeps his state,
Smiles to behold with what slow feet he moves.
Move slower, gentlier yet, O Time! or find
A way to fix her here, bound by our filial loves.

WILLIAM CALDWELL ROSCOE, 1823-1859

PORTRAIT OF THE ARTIST'S MOTHER.
JAMES ABBOT MCNEILL WHISTLER (1834-1903)
Musée D'Orsay, Paris.

Index